Embracing Your Gay: The Power of Freedom & Expression

Are you gay? Do you think you might be gay, but have yet to figure that out for sure? If you find yourself either questioning your sexuality or certain that you are not straight, then it is time to learn how to embrace your gay. With the help of this book, you will soon be well on your way to loving yourself for who you are, and accepting every part of your life, from the inside out. You will learn everything there is to know about how to be yourself, and you will never again find yourself lost without a way to show off your personal identity.

But what does embracing your gay have to do with you? Some people may find that they have trouble accepting themselves, and especially accepting their sexualities. If you do not love yourself, including your sexual preferences, how can you be truly happy? If you hope to achieve happiness in your lifetime, it is important to embrace your gay.

Of course, you must first learn to discover your inner gay before you can do this. This book is here to help you learn how to come to terms with your gay self, and how to tell others about your personal identity, if you so choose. You can find plenty of tips here to help you deal with just about any response you might get from your friends and family, and encouragement for the situations where you do not want to come out.

In these pages, you will also find tons of information on how to keep yourself feeling empowered, even when times get hard. Unfortunately, being gay means that you may face a lot of oppression, marginalization, and negativity from the people in your life, as well as from strangers. This is not an easy journey, but accepting yourself for who you truly are and learning to express your real self openly are important steps toward achieving happiness. The more you work toward embracing your gay, the freer you will feel, and the more comfortable you will be with expressing yourself.

Read on to learn more about the power of being gay, and how you can be proud of yourself from the inside out.

Table of Contents

Chapter One – Finding Your Inner Gay

If you are just starting out on your journey toward embracing your gay and learning to be free and express yourself, you might still be a little bit concerned and confused. You may be pretty sure that you identify as gay, but realizing this and accepting it as a part of who you are can be very different things. It is a huge first step to admit to yourself that you are gay, and you cannot learn to embrace yourself until you truly begin your journey.

So how can you find your inner gay? There are many different ways you can go about discovering yourself on the inside so you can express yourself outwardly more freely. Go into this process with an open mind, and keep your heart open toward yourself as well. The more willing you are to be your true self, the easier it will be for you to find empowerment and strength in the lifestyle that makes you the happiest.

How to soul-search

Are you ready to begin looking for your inner gay? Soul-searching is a great way to get started. If you have already come to the conclusion that you are gay, you may not have to start from the ground up. Even so, it can be helpful to spend a little time thinking hard about yourself, your feelings, and your place in the world. This can be a daunting task, but with the right tips and tricks to help guide you, it will not be that difficult.

Get started on your soul-searching journey by practicing meditation. Even if you have never tried meditating before, this can be a great way to help you become mindful of yourself and get in touch with your own beliefs, feelings, and more. Meditating does not have to be difficult, and even beginners can learn quickly. Try these tips for meditating to help you find your inner gay:

- Sit in a quiet room without any distractions.
- Close your eyes and sit upright with good posture. You can cross your legs, but you do not have to.
- Breathe normally, and count your breaths in and out. For example, count one in, one out; two in, two out.
- Count to ten and try to keep your mind clear from any thoughts.
- If you lose count or get distracted thinking hard about something, simply start over.

Do this for around 20 minutes a day to help train your mind to calm down and think clearly. Soon, you will be able to think about yourself and your needs without feeling distracted by other problems.

If this method of meditation is not doing enough to help you figure yourself out, you can try an alternate style instead. First, try the breath counting meditation for a few days to get into the habit of calming your mind. From there, give these steps a try instead:

- Sit down with your eyes closed in a quiet space.
- Think about a single problem you would like to work on. Do not get caught up in the bigger picture, but narrow down the problem to its source.
- For example, focus on something like "I am gay, and that worries me," instead of a bigger problem like "I am gay, and I'm afraid of what society will say to me, and how my family will react, and how I should behave."
- Keep this thought in your mind as you breathe in and out slowly and open your eyes.
- Pick a point on the wall or an object around the room, and stare at it as you think about your problem.
- Let all other thoughts, sights, sounds, and worries fade away. Simply think on your problem, and see how it makes you feel.

Spend 20 minutes a day doing this to help you organize your feelings, beliefs, and morals, and to give you a chance to uncover some useful ideas about yourself and your sexuality.

This is not a choice

Remember, while you are soul-searching, that this is not a choice. In the past, it was often thought that being gay was completely optional, and that gay people could always change at the drop of a hat. This is simply not true, and you are doing nothing but hurting yourself if you attempt to believe that you have any say in your sexuality. You are who you are, and your sexuality is what it is. Nothing you have chosen or avoided in your life can change that, and you should not expect it to.

You would not choose something that might cause you harm or put you in danger, would you? If you are gay, remember that this is a part of you, just like the color of your skin or the shape of your face is a part of you. If you could choose your sexuality, you probably would not go with one that has been marginalized, oppressed, and targeted in hate crimes. This is plenty of evidence to prove to yourself that there is nothing you can do to change who you are.

Accept yourself

When you realize that this is not a choice and that you cannot change your sexuality, the last step toward finding your inner gay is to accept yourself. At some point, you have to sit down and say to yourself, "I'm gay, and I accept this." The longer you avoid letting yourself be who you truly are, the more you will hurt and suffer.

Being gay is not always easy, and sometimes, there is more suffering to be found along the road toward a freer you. When you accept yourself for who you truly are, however, you can face whatever comes your way with an open mind and a sense of understanding that will help you feel empowered by your inner self, instead of held back. Keep reading to find out what to do once you are able to accept yourself, and how to work toward expressing yourself in the way that feels right to you.

Chapter Two – Stereotypes and You

Stereotypes are a huge part of gay culture. Unfortunately, stereotypes can also often be very hurtful, and they can cause a lot more harm than good. Many stereotypes have been designed by people outside the gay community, and they are used to make fun of, belittle, or emotionally target gay people on a daily basis. You might even come across some of these stereotypes in the media, where they have become so widely accepted that most people do not even realize how harmful it is to spread these kinds of ideas. A lot of gay stereotypes date back to a time well before being openly gay was as prominent as it is today, and this means that they are outdated ideas that need to be changed.

Do I have to fit into stereotypes?

If you have recently admitted to yourself that you are gay, worrying about stereotypes can be a major detriment to your journey toward self-acceptance and expression. You may have heard, for example, that gay men should all speak a certain way or be incredibly promiscuous all the time. You might have heard that gay women have to wear plaid shirts constantly and try their best to look like men. You might have even heard that gay people are usually poor, or trashy, or any number of other hurtful comments. Remember that stereotypes are not true, and that just because you identify as gay does not mean that you suddenly have to start looking or acting a certain way to be accepted.

As a matter of fact, most gay people do not fit into these stereotypes at all. You might have encountered several gay people in your daily life without even knowing it. Gay men can speak however they want to, and they do not have to be out for sex all the time. Gay women can wear any kind of clothing they like, and can be as feminine as they choose, too. And of course, gay people can come from any walk of life, from any social and economic class, and from any neighborhood. Just like straight people do not have to fit into certain groups or look a certain way to be who they are, neither do you.

What if I want to?

It is a different story altogether if you want to fit into these stereotypes, but it is important to be sure you make this decision for the right reason. Let us use the example of gay women wearing plaid and looking masculine. If you are a gay woman, it is well within your right to wear whatever you want. If you like to wear plaid, by all means, express yourself the way you feel most comfortable! If you like to cut your hair short, never wear makeup, and dress in baggy clothes, you can do that as well. No one can tell you what to do with your body or how to express yourself.

However, be sure you are not doing this simply because you think you have to. Think about your personal style, and how you feel comfortable dressing on a daily basis. Do you actually enjoy wearing makeup, but feel like you are somehow no longer allowed to put it on because you are gay? Or do you hate dealing with it and find yourself not caring whether or not your face looks a certain way every time you step outside? Gay men and women both should always remember to express themselves the way they see fit, whether that expression is part of a stereotype or not.

What about gender stereotypes?

Gender identity and sexuality are two different topics, and your gender identity does not have to go hand in hand with being gay. You can be gay and transgendered, for example, since these two identities are not mutually exclusive. However, there are a few stereotypes that may cause you some grief when you are trying to embrace your gay.

For example, if you are a gay man who enjoys hobbies like cooking, sewing, or shopping, you may feel pressured to hide these traits when you are around your straight male friends. Society often expects men to like sports, enjoy working with tools or fixing cars, and avoid hobbies that might make them seem somehow "less masculine." Remember that your hobbies are just as important a part of you as anything else, and that you should never feel pressured to do something you do not enjoy doing.

On the other hand, if you do like more masculine hobbies, that does not make you any less gay. You are who you are, and you like what you like, no matter what. Embracing your gay is easy when you remember that there is nothing wrong with any aspect of who you are, and that expressing yourself and your interests the way you like best is the most important thing you can do for yourself. Hobbies do not really have a gender, anyway!

Chapter Three – Telling Others

Telling others about your sexuality is a huge step toward embracing your inner gay. It is important to tell others about your identity when you feel like the time is right. Keeping it to yourself for the rest of your life is not a good way to feel better about yourself, and there is no empowerment in feeling like you have to hide an integral part of who you are. When you tell other people about your sexual identity, you are sharing with them a deep secret that helps you connect with them and express yourself at the same time.

When you are ready

First and foremost, remember that you never have to tell anyone about your identity until you feel ready. Never rush into this kind of conversation, even if you feel as though the person you are telling will be completely understanding. You should always arm yourself with plenty of information to help you anticipate any kind of reaction you might get from your friends and family. This way, no matter what happens, you can be prepared to face the outcome.

You can find other ways to embrace your gay and feel empowered and expressive without having to tell everyone in your life right away. Although eventually it will be important for you to let everyone know, regardless of how they might react, you do not have to take this step right away. Spend some time considering your options, and thinking about how you want to tell the people you care about. Do not wait so long, however, that it is impossible to bring yourself to say anything about it at all. You will know the right time to talk to your friends and family about your sexuality. Until then, learn how to prepare for just about anything they might say back to you.

Negativity from loved ones

Unfortunately, not everyone is going to be as accepting as you would like when you first come out to them. It can be very hard to hear someone you love say something negative or harsh to you when you open up and share such a deep secret. Preparing yourself for negativity is a key factor in getting through difficult conversations with loved ones.

Remind yourself, before you ever begin your conversation, that there is no guarantee as to how your loved one will respond. You might be surprised, for worse or better, by the reaction you get. Remember, too, that no matter what happens, the person you speak to may need some time to get used to the idea of you being gay. This does not make you any less valid of an individual, and it does not mean that you are not gay, even if your friends or family cannot accept it.

Accepting yourself is what matters. Telling others is important when it comes to feeling great about who you are inside, but their acceptance or rejection does not define you. You are a powerful, strong person no matter what they say.

Religious complaints

One of the biggest complaints you are likely to hear from your family or friends is that being gay is against their religion. If you were raised to be religious, this could be doubly difficult to hear, since you might not want to change your beliefs just because of your sexuality. There is no real reason why you cannot be a part of the religion of your choice and still be gay. Many churches and places of worship from all kinds of different religions are beginning to accept gay members in their congregations. It is becoming easier every day to find a place to practice the religion of your choice without your sexuality being called into question.

Things may be a little bit more difficult if you are not religious, but your friends or family are. You might find yourself hounded constantly by people who believe they are doing something right in telling you that you are sinning. In these situations, remember that many religious texts are both outdated and open to interpretation, and that it is impossible to say that being gay is a sin according to most of these documents. Your friends and family are entitled to their beliefs, and so are you. In the end, pretending to be something you are not just because an ancient text says you should is not a healthy way to live, and you can never feel empowered that way.

Expectation to change

Another common response you are likely to hear from your family and friends is an expectation to change. When you come out to them, they may immediately say something they think is helpful, such as, "That's okay, you can change." Even if they mean well when they say something like this, it can be hurtful to feel as though your sexuality has been completely invalidated by someone you love. Your family and friends may think that you can change if they explain to you why they think being gay is wrong, but it is important to stand strong against this kind of response. Even a response that is meant well can still be very negative and hurtful, and you are not in the wrong if you do not want to hear it.

You should never have to feel like you need to change who you are to be accepted. If your friends or family expect you to change before they can appreciate your identity, then they are not worth your time or effort. When they see that you are very serious about this part of yourself, they will slowly warm up to the idea that this is not going away. Eventually, with time and patience, they are likely to accept you. In the meantime, you can work on accepting yourself, and remembering that no one else's expectations can define you.

Take things slowly

The most important thing to remember when planning to tell others about your sexuality is to take it slowly. You do not have to call up everyone you have ever known as soon as you learn to accept your inner gay. You can slowly embrace yourself from the inside out by telling people one or two at a time, until your circle of support grows larger.

Start by telling a couple of people you can really trust. These may or may not be your parents, siblings, or best friend. You might really need to take a moment to consider the people who are more likely to respond well to you coming out to them. Even if you are very close with your parents, for example, they might be old-fashioned and think that being gay is something to be ashamed of, or something to "fix." A close friend or trustworthy sibling might be a better choice.

Eventually, you can work your way up to telling more people. When you have a few successful conversations under your belt, you are sure to feel better about handling the ones that may not end quite as well. Best of all, the friends and family you have already told can offer moral support for the times when you need to come out to someone less understanding. You might even find it more helpful to bring along a friend or two when you plan to have this conversation with those who might not take it as well.

Remember that telling others is a key step toward accepting yourself and expressing your identity the way you feel is right. You cannot love your inner self until you are able to share that self with others.

Chapter Four – Finding Support

Embracing your gay is much easier when you have a great support system to help back you up. Unfortunately, many gay people today do not have anyone to lean on when things get difficult, and this leads to tragic endings in some cases. It is important to be able to trust the people you talk to on a regular basis, and to get away from those who might hurt you or make you doubt yourself. If the people you associate with are not actively helping you embrace yourself and express your identity the way you want to, then they are not worth keeping in your life. Cutting ties can be difficult, but it is sometimes necessary to move forward with a better support system.

Join groups

Being a part of a group is a great way to network and get a support system started right away. When you find a group to join, you are already well on your way to making new friends and acquaintances who can help you out with every step of your journey. Finding a support group is a great way to get started. In a support group, you have the benefit of getting to know people who have already been through part of your path to personal empowerment, and who can act as mentors to you in times of need. In turn, you can offer support to others who might be looking for a friend to help them get through their struggles.

Groups do not have to be limited to support groups, however. Sometimes, just getting involved in a fun group with other gay individuals can be the best thing for your road to self empowerment. Look for groups in your area that get together and have parties, eat at great local restaurants, or participate in sports you enjoy. This way, you never have to feel pressured to talk about your experiences if you do not want to, but you can still reach out to other gay people and find a few friends along the way.

If you do not have any local groups, head to the Internet to find like-minded gay people to get to know. You do not have to go to dating sites for this! Look for discussion forums and social media groups where gay people hang out online. This is an even better way to reach out if you are a shy person, or if you do not feel safe enough to let your local loved ones know you are gay by participating in groups in your area.

Do not expect support

It is human nature to expect your friends and family to be supportive. However, you are doing yourself a disservice if you go into your journey toward embracing your gay expecting everyone to suddenly support you. This can only lead you to feeling let down in the long run, when someone in your life inevitably says something hurtful or otherwise does not support you. You cannot expect everyone you know to be supportive from day one, and that is okay. Just remember that even though it is alright for the people in your life to choose not to support you, that does not mean you have to waste time trying to make them accept you.

Refer to the previous chapter for tips on how to deal with those times when your support system is weak. It can be difficult trying to embrace your gay identity when your home life and circle of friends seem to be shutting you down at every opportunity. This is the unfortunate reality of the lives of many gay people, but do not worry. Even if you find yourself in this situation, you need only reach out to local groups to find friends that can help you every step of the way.

Forgiveness is key

When someone you love refuses to accept you because you are gay, it can hurt quite a lot. It may take a long time to bounce back from something like that, but you can practice forgiveness to help yourself feel better. It takes a lot to want to forgive someone who has wronged you in the past, and if you do not feel like you can forgive at first, that is okay. Take your time, and calm down before you think about the situation again.

If it does nothing else, forgiveness can at least help you feel stronger in knowing that you are a bigger person than those who cannot accept you. You can feel strong and powerful when you realize that you are able to forgive the people who are too narrow-minded to accept you for who you are. This additional strength can, in turn, help you accept and love yourself, and give you the confidence you need to be the person you really are, even in the face of difficulties.

Be yourself on the outside

Outwardly showing your gay identity is a great way to find support. It can be tough finding the confidence to be openly gay in public, but when you finally overcome that hurdle, you will find new friends and areas of support pouring in from places you might never have expected. When you come out to your friends, you might find that you are not alone, and that some of the people you have known for years are gay as well. Even if this does not happen, you might end up connecting through friends with other gay people, and expanding your support system this way instead.

You can support yourself by being more open about your sexual identity, as well. When you are free and open with your self-expression, you are much more likely to feel good about yourself and your life. Being who you want to be on the outside can make you feel amazing on the inside, and in turn, feeling great about your identity can help you project more strength and confidence outwardly. Keep yourself fighting strong by showing off your inner gay on the outside sometimes, too.

Cut out toxic people

Maybe the most important step in improving your support system is cutting out the toxic people in your life. It can be very hard to let go of connections you have had for years, especially when you care deeply about the people you know. Unfortunately, in some cases it is necessary to get rid of negativity by cutting ties with the toxic people who cause it. Toxic people are different from those who simply do not understand or who need a little time to come to terms with your identity. When someone is toxic, that person goes out of their way to make you feel bad about yourself, to insult you or put you down, or to make you believe there is something wrong with you.

The best way to get a toxic person out of your life is to do it quickly. Tell the person that you do not want to have anything to do with them anymore, and then cut it off there. Do not give them a chance to come back into your life again, because it is very likely they will repeat the same behavior again and again. If the toxic person is a member of your family, you may still have to encounter that individual from time to time, but you can practice letting your inner gay empowerment shine by holding your head up high and not letting them get to you.

Chapter Five – Overcoming Pressure and Marginalization

Marginalization is the concept of treating a group of people as if they do not matter, or as if they are an afterthought to a more important group. Many different minority groups can be marginalized, based on skin color, economic status, beliefs, and of course, sexuality or gender identity. This is a common problem throughout the world when it comes to gay people and couples, and unfortunately, the United States has a lot of issues with marginalizing the gay community even in the modern world.

If you do not find yourself a victim of large-scale community marginalization, count yourself lucky. In many local cities and neighborhoods, gay people are shunned and seen as something wrong that should not be allowed to live among heterosexuals. This is a terrible way of thinking, but when you are not comfortable with yourself, it can be impossible to look past it. You must learn to love yourself so that you can become a shining example to those around you. The more you embrace yourself, the easier it will be for others to learn to accept you as well.

Marginalization comes in many forms

Gay people have been marginalized and ostracized from their communities for centuries. Although the punishment for being gay is much less harsh today than it was long ago, very old traditions and beliefs unfortunately still remain prevalent throughout society. Early Christian religious documentation reveals that, in the 18th century, people who were found to be gay were burned at the stake or otherwise put to death. Thankfully, the United States does not hold those kinds of barbaric views any longer, but marginalization comes in many different forms.

Over time, the death penalty for homosexuality was lifted, but modern day governments still crack down on gay individuals and couples by refusing to allow them the same benefits and privileges that straight people receive. Although being gay is no longer seen as a mental illness, it is still viewed as a sin or as something unnatural by far too many people in positions of power. Because of this, hate crimes are still prominent against members of the gay community, and you may find yourself on the receiving end of more than one angry outburst when you embrace your gay outwardly.

Only since 2000 have conditions slowly started to change. Now, the United States finally allows same sex couples to have the same benefits as heterosexual couples, and gay marriage is recognized and legal throughout the entire country. Gay marriage has only been legal in the whole United States since 2015, which just goes to show that marginalization is still a very real problem. It is important to be prepared for oppression when you embrace your gay, but to also remember that you are a valuable and valid person who deserves to be happy and free. Never let these kinds of pressures keep you from being yourself.

Behaving in public

With so many problems with oppression and marginalization coming from every direction, you may catch yourself wondering how you are supposed to behave in public. Should you hide yourself away and only open up with people you can completely trust, or should you show your gay side every chance you get? To make the most out of your newly empowered lifestyle, it is better if you find a happy medium between these two extremes.

It is important to keep from making a big scene when you are in a public place. There is nothing wrong with showing affection toward your partner or even talking about your gay life with your friends and family in public. However, you should always know where to draw the line. Being yourself and openly embracing your inner gay identity is an excellent practice in any situation, but going to the trouble to draw attention to yourself in a place where you know this could cause trouble is a bad idea. Do not go into a situation filled with anti-gay fanatics and loudly proclaim yourself—this will not end well.

That is not to say you should never be yourself in public. You never have to be ashamed of who you are and what makes you such a unique individual. Keeping safe and refraining from causing a scene is not the same thing as hiding yourself away completely. When you are in a public place that is not judgmental or dangerous, there is no reason why you cannot openly be yourself. Dress the way you want to, flirt a little, and have fun. The more open you can be in public, the happier you will be in your day to day life.

Fighting back against marginalization

There are many different ways you can fight back against marginalization in your day to day life. If pressure comes from the people close to you, including your family, friends, or local community, you can practice standing up for yourself more and more each time this happens. It can be tempting to just quietly accept the harsh words and nasty jokes people might say about you, but this is the worst way to respond. Without becoming unpleasant yourself, simply remind those around you that this was not a choice for you, and that you are embracing yourself and accepting your life as it is.

On a larger scale, you can help reduce marginalization in your city, state, and country by joining groups that spread awareness and visibility of gay people and couples. Join parades, walks, and marathons, or volunteer for organizations that peacefully educate and inform communities about gay rights. The more you get involved, the better you will feel about yourself, and you will be able to embrace your inner identity that much more easily.

No matter how you fight, changes start within you. Embrace your gay and be proud of who you are. You will be empowered to battle injustice and prejudice frequently with the strength of self-acceptance to back you up.

Chapter Six – Personal Hurdles Along the Way

While many problems you might face on your journey to embracing your inner gay may come from the outside, several can come from the inside as well. When you lose sight of your goals of empowerment and self-appreciation, you can easily get inside your own head and make yourself feel worthless or problematic. This happens to everyone at some point along their path, but you can be on the lookout for this pitfall of negativity by arming yourself with the information you need to get through it.

Internal problems

Problems do not always come from the outside. External issues are common when you come out as gay, but internal troubles arise just as quickly. Sometimes, it may be tough to figure out whether or not your problems are created by yourself or by your environment. You may project feelings of shame and dislike onto your friends and family, when in actuality, they are trying to accept you for who you are. Negative feelings often come from within, and when this happens, it is necessary to learn how to deal with them.

When you can recognize your problems as internal ones, you have already made an important first step toward healing your emotions and embracing yourself. Take a step back every time you have a negative thought about yourself and your identity, and try to determine where that thought stems from. Does it come from something another person said about you, or did you really think it about yourself? If this kind of negativity comes from within, it is time to learn how to move past it.

Overcoming guilt

Guilt comes in many forms, and it can be a tough hurdle to jump. If you were raised to believe that being gay is unnatural, sinful, or wrong in some other way, you are much more likely to develop feelings of guilt and self-punishment. You may believe that you are irredeemable, and that you can never learn how to accept yourself because you are so "wrong." Guilt is a self-made concept, and you can learn to move beyond it toward a firmer acceptance and understanding of your real self.

Learning to control your guilt and remembering your ultimate goal is difficult, but so worth it in the end. Remind yourself every day that your goal is to be empowered, inspired, enlightened, and accepting of yourself. This means every aspect of yourself—including those that may make you feel ashamed. You are a brilliant and wonderful individual, and you deserve respect from yourself as well as from those around you. Your sexuality is as much a part of you as your blood type, and you have nothing to feel guilty or ashamed for. Tell yourself this (aloud, if possible) every day, and over time, you will come to believe it.

Overcoming loneliness

When you embrace your gay identity and start living your life more openly, you might find yourself ostracized from the people you once loved the most. This can be a very isolating and lonely feeling. You may start going through the motions of daily life without really enjoying yourself, and this is a major detriment to your journey toward self-expression and personal acceptance.

Loneliness is a huge problem in the gay community, but it does not have to affect you. Refer to Chapter Four to learn more about finding support in your local community, and about how to find online groups as well. Feeling desperately lonely can make you depressed and uninterested in reaching out to find others. This is a vicious cycle, so break out of it by forcing yourself to look for involvement a little bit every day. The more you search for other like-minded people, the happier you will be. Every new connection is another step toward embracing your gay.

Exploring your sexuality

One great way to get in touch with your inner self is to safely explore your own sexuality. This does not mean hooking up with the first person you meet at a party, but it does mean being brave enough to read or watch adult entertainment in the right situations. If you live with family or friends who would not approve, take caution with this step. And of course, if you are not an adult, you will have to wait a little while before you can reach this crucial point in accepting your sexual identity.

It is not easy for everyone to jump into exploring their sexuality, and some of you will have to work on getting over your nerves and your guilt before you reach this point. Remember that this a necessary step toward understanding yourself. It is perfectly natural to be a sexual person, and to want to know what gets you excited. Stay safe when exploring your new identity, but do not be afraid to try something new. You never know when you might find just the right activity that tips the scale and helps you be more accepting of yourself in the long run.

You are never alone

Even when things look bleak, remember that you are never alone. There is always someone going through the same kinds of experience as you, and most of the time, they are no more than a few web sites or phone calls away. You may feel like the only gay person in your city, but that is very likely not true either. Getting inside your own head and feeling sad, depressed, or alone hurts, but you can always get through it. In this modern era, you need only check out social media to find someone to talk to at any time of the day or night.

You are not different, wrong, or weird for being gay. You are yourself, and you are worthwhile and valuable. Start every morning and go to bed every night reminding yourself of this. It might be hard to believe at first, especially if you have had a difficult journey to get to this point. The more you say it, the more likely you are to believe it, and soon you will become a beacon of self-love and personal appreciation among your local community. Others will respect you more when you respect yourself, and you will be stronger than ever before when you overcome these hurdles of doubt and loneliness.

Chapter Seven – Figuring Out Where You Fit In

Once you come to terms with accepting yourself and learn how to respond when others react negatively toward your personal empowerment, you can figure out where you fit in. The gay community is vast and welcoming, and there are many different ways you can determine how to become a part of it. The options are only limited by your own preferences. Remember that you do not have to make yourself do anything you do not want to do, and you are not required to fit into any specific "standards" for being gay. Figuring out where you fit into your identity is one of the most rewarding parts of exploring yourself.

Be as open as you like

The more you appreciate yourself and your inner gay identity, the more comfortable you will become with being openly gay in public places. As you progress on your journey toward gay empowerment, you will feel more and more like telling everyone you know about who you are. This is normal, and as long as you will not be in a dangerous situation, go ahead and tell the world! Be as open as you want to be, but remember that your gay authenticity is not defined by how open you are.

if you choose not to be as openly gay as some of your friends or other community connections, that is okay as well. The choice is yours. Just remember that it is important to be open whenever possible, at least with the people you can trust. You will never make much progress on the path toward embracing yourself if you feel unsafe being yourself. Every time you go to a gathering with your local gay friends or join a chat or online group, work on being a little bit more open about who you are. Every step matters, even if it is a small one. The more open you are, the happier you will be about your identity.

Be religious if you choose

There is nothing that says you cannot be both gay and religious. Many religions today have made modern changes that include accepting gay members, and even in some cases, gay leaders. If religion is a big part of who you are, you can still fit into the gay community without ever having to give up this side of yourself. There are plenty of religious gay people all across the United States today. You may need to look a little harder to find these kinds of groups, but they are definitely out there.

If religion does not matter much to you, there is no need to feel pressured into being religious, no matter who you are. Your family cannot make you follow a religious path, and they cannot decide that being gay is a sin, either. You are welcome to be a part of both the gay and religious communities in your area, but you are not obligated to blend the two if you do not feel comfortable doing so. Some parts of the country are still backwards in this way, and you may want to distance yourself from religion in order to avoid unwanted conflict in your town.

Find a mentor

When you first start out on your journey toward self-acceptance, you might need a little help embracing your gay and being yourself. Finding a mentor is a great way to learn what it really is to be gay and love every moment of it. A mentor can be anyone who has been a part of the gay community for longer than you have, and who can answer questions and give you that extra boost of confidence you need to keep learning about yourself and your personal identity.

When you have a mentor, you automatically have a connection to help you figure out where you belong among other like-minded people. Your mentor might be interested in a certain aspect of the local gay community that might pique your interests as well. On the other hand, even if you do not share the same hobbies or personal choices, your mentor might know how to put you in contact with someone even more like you. You may not find someone to be an "official" mentor, but any trustworthy fellow gay friend can fill this role.

Become a mentor

After you have been a part of the gay community for a while yourself, you might want to become a mentor to someone else. Your personal experiences are unique and valid, and you might have some support or words of wisdom to offer another person going through the same things you once had to deal with. Your struggles can become inspiration for someone else. You never know when someone who has recently accepted himself or herself might be looking to you for guidance.

Becoming a mentor may be exactly where you belong in the gay community. The more you embrace your gay and learn about yourself, the more connections you will make with other people in your area and online, as well. You might get to know newly out gay individuals or couples looking to make a friend, and you might even get involved with local outreach. The possibilities are endless.

Defend yourself and your community

It may take you years to figure out what part of the gay community you fit into, and there is nothing wrong with that. You cannot jump immediately from accepting yourself to knowing the roles you want to play and the way you want to present yourself to the public. It takes time to get to this point, and you might even make the wrong call a few times along the way. You might decide you are into the night life and club scene, only to later realize that what you really want is to get involved with outreach and awareness causes. Who knows? Only you can figure out how to be a part of the gay community. With time, effort, and plenty of self-appreciation, you will eventually find your place.

Even while you are exploring where you fit in, you can do a lot to defend yourself and your community against problems that might arise. You become a part of a larger group as soon as you accept yourself as being gay. The longer you openly live your life and show the world who you really are, the more firmly you cement yourself as one of a huge number of other gay people throughout the country and around the world. When something happens to affect your community, you should always be ready to react. Your personal empowerment can be a valuable asset toward reaching out and making a difference against oppression.

Chapter Eight – Freeing Yourself

You have come a long way from the beginning of this book, and from the start of your journey as well. The steps along the path toward freeing your inner gay self are many and varied, and the struggles are different from person to person. Your experiences may not match those of other people you know or meet along the way, but everything that happens to you and everything you feel is valid. You are an authentic, beautiful individual with a personality and identity all your own. Opening your heart and living your life the way that makes you feel most comfortable is freeing, and in turn, freeing yourself can give you the kind of empowerment you never thought possible.

Being gay is being free

Did you know that being gay is being free? You might not feel like this is true when you face discrimination at every turn, but the more you work through your life and overcome these kinds of obstacles, the more you will realize just how free you have become. No longer are you tied down to unhealthy traditions and old-fashioned ways of thinking. Now that you are openly gay, you are free to be yourself in every sense of the word, and to express your individuality in new and amazing ways every day.

Be individual without being alone

When you are free, you can accept yourself and discover your own personal individuality. You are able to try new things, get out there and get involved with new people, and figure out what makes you happy. You can become more confident in everything that you do, knowing that your decisions are backed by your freedom and your constant goal to be yourself and enjoy your life to its fullest.

Do not go so far into making yourself individual that you distance yourself from the rest of the gay community, however. It is important to be a part of the community and to know what you like and enjoy doing, but if you try too hard to stand out from the crowd, it may be more difficult for you to make friends. Be yourself and enjoy the hobbies, activities, and preferences you truly like best. Do not force yourself or pretend to be something you are not. Even if you feel like you are doing the right thing by trying to be "gay enough," you are really hurting yourself. All you have to do is be the real you, and the rest will come naturally.

Accept others

As you become more willing to express yourself and accept your feelings, you will be faced with more and more chances to accept others as well. Loving yourself is the first step toward having an open heart and mind toward the people you meet every day. In turn, when you can freely accept others for who they are, you will feel better about yourself, and your confidence and strength will increase. Keep treating other people with respect, and you will get that back every time.

In some unfortunate cases, self-expression and empowerment lead to egotism and elitism among the gay community. Every group has its problematic members, and the gay community is no different. Just because someone is gay does not mean they are automatically a great person, but you can strive to be good to other people by avoiding these negative feelings toward those you come into contact with. Remember that the way you express yourself is no better than the way someone else does, and that just because you feel more empowered than another person does not give you the right to put them down for their own experiences. We are all in this together, and we can give strength to each other by treating each other well.

Never suppress your self-expression

When you live with or near family or friends who make you feel like being yourself is wrong, it is hard to want to express yourself openly. Self-expression is a very important part of embracing your gay and being strong and powerful from the inside out. Even if you can only express your identity in little ways at first, these are crucial steps toward building up more and more confidence in who you truly are.

When you suppress your self-expression, you set yourself back significantly. You have come so far to be able to accept yourself, and to learn what you enjoy and where you fit into the rest of the community. Now is not the time to be shy! Be true to yourself in every aspect of your life. Do not lie about your sexuality, and do not pretend to be something other than what you truly are. Your sexuality does not have to define you, but you should always be willing to let it be known when the time is right.

Free yourself by fighting back

Freeing yourself and your identity is even easier when you get involved in local and worldwide efforts to make things better for everyone. The more often you work toward the greater good of gay people everywhere, the better you will feel about yourself. This is a great confidence booster to help you love every part of yourself. You will feel freer and happier every time you give back to your cause.

Chapter Nine – A More Open America

You have learned to accept yourself. You have admitted to yourself that you are gay, and with effort, you have come to love this part of yourself and understand that it is not a choice, but who you really are. You have told the people in your life who matter the most, and you have learned who you can really trust by coming out slowly. You may have even found groups of friends, support systems, and more in your community or online. You have done everything you can to empower yourself and set yourself up for success in your incredible gay life.

Now what? Now it is time to put your new personal strength to good use. Make your power known, and make your voice heard by fighting back against the problems of marginalization, oppression, discrimination and prejudice that still linger in the United States and around the world. Things are still hard for gay people like yourself, and you can make a difference. Let your inner gay be as free as possible as you find new ways to challenge yourself and the rest of the world.

Fighting laws and regulations

Just because gay marriage is legal in the United States does not mean that everyone automatically accepts it. Unfortunately, in many states, laws are being passed or attempted that give specific counties and cities the right to deny marriage licenses to gay couples looking to get married. This is unconstitutional, but it is still happening, and fighting back against these kinds of proposals is a great way to get involved.

Although sexuality and gender identity are not the same issue, the gay community has recently been helping take a stand against bathroom bills that keep transgendered individuals from using the restrooms in which they feel most comfortable. Gender and sexuality go hand in hand, so even though they are not the same issue, there is a sense of solidarity between the two communities. You can do a lot of good for human rights by helping fight against bathroom bills as well.

Remember to always wage your battles as peacefully as possible, to avoid bringing more harm than good to the community at large. Write letters of protest, join picket lines and other peaceful demonstrations, and go to the media when possible to shed some light on the injustices that are still happening all over the country. Social media has made a major difference in many of these issues in the past couple of years, so never be afraid to reach out online for help when you see something that goes against your sense of what is right and just.

Looking to the future

In the United States, gay marriage was finally legalized in 2015, but this is only the beginning. Legal marriages were never the end game in the gay rights movement. Although this is an excellent step, and one that should be celebrated, it is not enough to make gay people and couples equal in the eyes of society, or in the eyes of the government. There are still so many more causes to fight for in the future, and so much discrimination to work on removing from our society, that you will probably never run out of causes to work toward.

In the future, the gay community as a whole can fight for equal rights in the eyes of insurance companies, employers, and even healthcare professionals who believe that it is fine to refuse service to someone just because of his or her sexuality. These injustices are important, and must be addressed. You can work toward bringing visibility to these problems and encouraging the public to support you and your fellow gay individuals, or you can choose one of the other areas in which gay rights need to be protected.

You may not realize it, but the media has a huge impact on gay rights visibility in the United States. One of the biggest ways you can help improve society's view of gay people like yourself is to focus on the media. Contact the people in charge of your favorite movies, television series, or channels, and draw attention through social media outlets to the lack of gay representation in the media. Although more gay people have been included in recent shows and movies, many times, the gay characters in these stories end up dying by the end of the plot. Strides have been made to include gay characters, but they are still not represented the same way as heterosexual characters in most instances. Over time, the media can help shape the public's view of gay rights and issues, and you can help motivate the media by writing letters and boycotting when necessary.

There are many other steps you can take to improve the quality of life for the gay people of the future. Bring your strength and empowerment to every letter you write and every protest you attend, and allow the confidence you have built throughout your journey to embracing your identity to shine through in everything that you do. You will be making a difference in the world in no time.

A more open world

If you do not want to get involved trying to make changes in the media or on the local level, you might want to widen your scope to a worldwide level instead. The world is a huge place, and although the United States is nowhere near being as welcoming and accepting as some countries, others are much more backward and set in harmful traditions. In some countries, being gay is still punishable by death, torture, and other brutal, barbaric means. Many gay people still live in fear for their lives and the lives of the people they love the most, and this is unforgivable.

So many people around the world have to suffer for being who they are. When you reach a point in your journey toward self-appreciation in which you are ready to help others on a massive scale, reach out to organizations that are trying to make a difference around the world. You may not think you are able to make much of a change, but one lone voice can join with thousands of others to be heard. You are an empowered, bright, and strong individual, and you know who you are. You love yourself, and you love and accept others too. Bring that confidence and sense of self-worth to your work in the gay community, and you may soon see yourself making changes at the global level. When you work toward these kinds of incredible goals, you may not believe what you can accomplish.

Conclusion

Are you ready to be the best you can be, from your inner gay to your outer expression of yourself? There are many steps you can take toward empowering yourself and feeling great about who you are. Whether you are just starting out on a path of self-exploration, you are looking for a way to tell the people you love about your identity, or you are just hoping to bring a new level of personal growth into your openly gay lifestyle, embracing your gay can help you love yourself and live a successful, happy life.

So what are you waiting for? It is time to get out there and show your pride!

www.ingramcontent.com/pod-product-compliance
Lightning Source LLC
Chambersburg PA
CBHW060820290526
45792CB00005BB/1734